So, you want to get a dog?

Your Guide to Choosing the Right Companion and Becoming a Responsible Owner.

Majella Gee

So, you want to get a dog?

© 2024 by Majella Gee
All rights reserved.

SORJAM
PUBLISHING

Published by Sorjam Publishing
Sunshine Coast Hinterland, Australia

This eBook is licensed for your personal enjoyment only. It may not be re-sold or given away to others. If you would like to share this book with someone else, please purchase an additional copy for each recipient. If you are reading this book and did not purchase it, or it was not purchased for your use only, please return to your preferred eBook retailer and purchase your own copy. Thank you for respecting the hard work of this author.

ISBN: 978-1-7636631-2-1
First Edition

About the Author

Growing up surrounded by pets, Majella's passion for animals and their care evolved into a lifelong dedication to their well-being. Early experiences of caring for pets at home and working at the local pet store during school holidays set the foundation for her future career in the pet industry.

Her expertise extends to a variety of animals. From managing pet shops where she cared for dogs, cats, birds, fish, reptiles, guinea pigs, and mice, her knowledge goes beyond companion animals. For decades, she has been a devoted wildlife carer, providing a safe haven and rehabilitation for numerous creatures.

Throughout her career, Majella has been a trusted advisor for pet owners, offering honest, practical advice. With a knack for identifying the perfect breed for a person's lifestyle, budget, and needs, she delves into details during consultations to determine the best match. She then guides individuals through the selection process and beyond, providing ongoing support.

Residing on the beautiful Sunshine Coast hinterland with her husband and rescue kitten Hank, she is surrounded by an abundance of wildlife. She continues to campaign for animal rights and supports numerous organizations, advocating for the rights of animals and supporting their rehabilitation and rehoming. Currently, Majella is writing a series of educational children's books, teaching responsible pet ownership to the next generation.

Ensuring that every pet finds the right home and receives the care they deserve is her lifelong mission.

Dedication

*To all the animals who have graced my life with their presence,
who have taught me more than I could ever learn from any book.
You have been my greatest teachers, my companions,
and the inspiration behind this journey.
This book is for you.*

Acknowledgments

To the loyal customers who became lifelong friends,
thank you for trusting me with your beloved pets
and for the shared stories that have enriched my life.

And to every animal I have had the privilege to care for,
you have shown me the true meaning of compassion,
patience, and unconditional love.

Every day, I continue to learn from you,
and every day, I will continue to be your voice.
May this book help others see the world through your eyes
and make a difference in the lives of all creatures,
great and small.

Table of Contents

Introduction	1
1. Choosing the Right Breed	3
2. Preparing Your Home	15
3. Essential Pre-Adoption Health Checks	20
4. Settling In – Helping your Dog Adjust to its New Home	25
5. Basic Training and Ongoing Education	30
6. Dogs and Children	35
7. Keeping your Dog Happy and Healthy	40
8. Signs of Illness and When to Seek Help	46
9. Recommended Reading and Resources	51
Conclusion	54

Introduction

Owning a dog is a commitment that goes beyond providing food and shelter; it's about ensuring a life filled with love, respect, and proper care. Unfortunately, many dogs end up in shelters or are mistreated because their owners were not fully prepared for the responsibility. This book aims to change that by offering a brutally honest guide to choosing the right dog and understanding the full scope of responsible pet ownership.

Every year, millions of dogs are abandoned, abused, or euthanized because their owners made uninformed decisions. The statistics are staggering and heartbreaking. In Australia, the RSPCA receives over 100,000 animals annually, with thousands being euthanized due to a lack of homes. In the US, around 3.3 million dogs enter shelters each year, and approximately 670,000 are euthanized. In the UK, the number of stray dogs is estimated at over 100,000 annually.

These numbers are not just statistics; they represent real animals who have suffered due to human negligence. This book aims to educate potential dog owners to prevent these tragedies. Choosing the right breed is crucial, as different breeds have different needs, temperaments, and potential health issues. Making an informed choice ensures a harmonious relationship between you and your dog, preventing the heartbreak of rehoming or worse.

1

Choosing the Right Breed

Choosing the right breed is the first and most crucial step in your journey to becoming a responsible dog owner. Different breeds have different needs, temperaments, and potential health issues. It's essential to match the breed to your lifestyle, environment, and family dynamics to ensure a harmonious relationship.

Herding Dogs

Characteristics: Herding dogs are known for their intelligence, trainability, and strong herding instincts. They excel in activities that require agility, obedience, and herding.

Common Breeds:

- Border Collie
- Australian Shepherd
- German Shepherd
- Collie
- Shetland Sheepdog
- Old English Sheepdog
- Corgi
- Australian Kelpie
- Hungarian Puli

Pros:

- Highly trainable and intelligent
- Excellent working dogs and family companions
- Loyal and protective

Cons:

- Require a lot of mental and physical stimulation
- Can be prone to herding behaviours in inappropriate settings
- High exercise needs can be demanding

Health Considerations:

- Hip Dysplasia: Common in larger herding breeds like German Shepherds.

- Eye Conditions: Border Collies may be prone to progressive retinal atrophy.

Hound Dogs

Characteristics: Hound dogs are bred for their hunting and tracking abilities. They have a keen sense of smell or sight, depending on the breed, and are often very independent.

Common Breeds:

- Beagle
- Bloodhound
- Greyhound
- Basset Hound
- Dachshund
- Afghan Hound
- American Foxhound
- Basenji
- Borzoi
- Irish Wolfhound
- Whippet
- Rhodesian Ridgeback

Pros:

- Excellent trackers and hunters
- Generally friendly and sociable
- Loyal and good with families

Cons:

- Can be stubborn and independent

- Require regular exercise to prevent boredom
- Prone to specific health issues related to their breed

Health Considerations:

- Ear Infections: Common in breeds with long ears like Basset Hounds.
- Back Issues: Dachshunds are prone to intervertebral disc disease.

Toy Dogs

Characteristics: Toy dogs are small in size and bred primarily for companionship. They adapt well to apartment living and require less space and exercise.

Common Breeds:

- Chihuahua
- Pomeranian
- Shih Tzu
- Yorkshire Terrier
- Pug
- Maltese
- Cavalier King Charles Spaniel
- Toy Poodle
- Papillon
- Havanese
- Italian Greyhound

Pros:

- Easy to carry and travel with
- Require less space and exercise

- Good for families in smaller living spaces

Cons:

- Can be fragile and prone to injury
- May be prone to barking and small dog syndrome
- Require socialization to prevent aggression

Health Considerations:

- Dental Issues: Common in small breeds due to overcrowded teeth.
- Luxating Patella: A common issue in toy breeds affecting the knee joint.

Non-Sporting Dogs

Characteristics: Non-sporting dogs are a diverse group with varying sizes, temperaments, and appearances. They were bred for a variety of purposes not related to hunting or herding.

Common Breeds:

- Bulldog
- Dalmatian
- Poodle
- Boston Terrier
- Bichon Frise
- French Bulldog
- Shiba Inu
- Chow Chow
- Lhasa Apso

- Tibetan Terrier
- Keeshond

Pros:

- Unique appearances and personalities
- Adaptable to various living conditions
- Good companions

Cons:

- Varied exercise and grooming needs depending on the breed
- Prone to specific health issues
- Temperaments can vary widely

Health Considerations:

- Skin Issues: Bulldogs can have skin fold infections.
- Deafness: Common in Dalmatians, requiring hearing tests.

Sporting Dogs

Characteristics: Sporting dogs are active and friendly, bred for hunting and retrieving. They excel in activities like swimming and love outdoor activities.

Common Breeds:

- Golden Retriever
- Labrador Retriever
- Cocker Spaniel
- English Setter

- Irish Setter
- Pointer
- Weimaraner
- Vizsla
- Brittany Spaniel
- Chesapeake Bay Retriever
- Springer Spaniel

Pros:

- Friendly and good with children
- Easy to train and eager to please
- Great companions for active families

Cons:

- Require regular exercise to prevent boredom and obesity
- Prone to certain health issues like hip dysplasia and ear infections
- Can be overly friendly with strangers

Health Considerations:

- Ear Infections: Common in breeds with floppy ears like Cocker Spaniels.
- Hip Dysplasia: A frequent issue in larger sporting breeds like Golden Retrievers.

Terrier Dogs

Characteristics: Terriers are known for their feisty and energetic nature. They were bred to hunt vermin and often display a strong prey drive.

Common Breeds:

- Jack Russell Terrier
- Scottish Terrier
- West Highland White Terrier
- Bull Terrier
- Airedale Terrier
- Cairn Terrier
- Border Terrier
- Staffordshire Bull Terrier
- American Pit Bull Terrier

Pros:

- Energetic and playful
- Good watchdogs
- Adapt well to various living conditions

Cons:

- Can be stubborn and challenging to train
- Require mental and physical stimulation
- May be aggressive towards other animals

Health Considerations:

- Skin Allergies: Common in breeds like Bull Terriers.
- Joint Issues: Terriers like Jack Russells can suffer from patellar luxation.

Working Dogs

Characteristics: Working dogs are large, strong, and bred for tasks like guarding, pulling sleds, and search and rescue.

They are intelligent and trainable but require a lot of exercise and mental stimulation.

Common Breeds:

- German Shepherd
- Rottweiler
- Boxer
- Siberian Husky
- Great Dane
- Doberman Pinscher
- Mastiff
- Saint Bernard
- Newfoundland
- Bernese Mountain Dog
- Akita

Pros:

- Highly trainable and intelligent
- Loyal and protective
- Excellent for specific tasks and jobs

Cons:

- Require significant exercise and mental stimulation
- Can be challenging to handle for inexperienced owners
- Prone to specific health issues related to their size

Health Considerations:

- Hip Dysplasia: Common in larger breeds like German Shepherds.
- Bloat: A serious condition in deep-chested breeds like Great Danes.

Crossbreeds

Crossbreeds are dogs with parents of different breeds. They can inherit traits from both parents, making them unique and sometimes unpredictable. Popular crossbreeds like Labradoodles and Cavoodles are often bred for specific traits, such as hypoallergenic coats, but it's essential to understand that crossbreeds can still have health issues and temperament challenges.

Characteristics:

- Unique combination of traits from both parent breeds
- Can be more adaptable and resilient
- Often marketed as hypoallergenic, but this is not always guaranteed

Common Crossbreeds:

- Labradoodle (Labrador Retriever x Poodle)
- Cavoodle (Cavalier King Charles Spaniel x Poodle)
- Puggle (Pug x Beagle)
- Cockapoo (Cocker Spaniel x Poodle)
- Maltipoo (Maltese x Poodle)
- Schnoodle (Schnauzer x Poodle)
- Goldendoodle (Golden Retriever x Poodle)

Pros:

- Potentially fewer hereditary health issues
- Unique and often appealing appearances
- Can be bred for specific traits, like hypoallergenic coats

Cons:

- Traits and temperaments can be unpredictable
- May still have health issues from both parent breeds
- Often expensive due to their trendy status

Choosing a Dog for Allergy-Prone People

For individuals with allergies, selecting a breed that sheds less or has hypoallergenic qualities is crucial. Allergens are typically found in a dog's dander, saliva, and urine, not just their fur. Breeds with hair instead of fur, or those that shed minimally, are often recommended for allergy sufferers.

Characteristics:

- Minimal shedding or hair instead of fur
- Regular grooming required to maintain coat
- May still produce allergens, so interaction with the breed before commitment is advised

Common Allergy-Friendly Breeds:

- Poodle
- Bichon Frise
- Maltese
- Shih Tzu
- Portuguese Water Dog
- Schnauzer
- Basenji
- Italian Greyhound
- Soft Coated Wheaten Terrier

Pros:

- Reduced allergen production
- Often have friendly and adaptable temperaments
- Good for families with allergy concerns

Cons:

- Regular grooming is essential
- No breed is completely hypoallergenic
- Individual reactions to breeds can vary

Health Considerations:

- Skin Issues: Some hypoallergenic breeds can have sensitive skin.
- Ear Infections: Regular grooming and cleaning are essential to prevent infections.

Exploring the diverse range of dog breeds can be an exciting and eye-opening journey. Each breed brings its own unique set of characteristics, needs, and potential health considerations. By taking the time to research and understand these differences, you can discover breeds that perfectly align with your lifestyle and preferences. Some breeds might surprise you with how well they fit into your family dynamic or living situation. Embrace this opportunity to learn about breeds you may not have heard of before and consider all your options carefully. An informed choice will lead to a rewarding and lasting relationship with your new furry friend.

2
Preparing Your Home

Before bringing your new dog home, it is essential to prepare your living environment to ensure it is safe, comfortable, and welcoming for your new companion. This preparation will help your dog settle in more smoothly and reduce the likelihood of accidents or issues arising. Proper preparation demonstrates your commitment to responsible pet ownership and sets the foundation for a harmonious relationship with your new dog.

The Importance of Preparing Your Home

Preparing your home before the arrival of your new dog is crucial. A well-prepared environment will make the transition easier for your dog and help establish a positive routine from day one. It also allows you to anticipate and mitigate potential hazards, creating a safe and stress-free space for your new pet.

Checklist for Preparation

1. **Sleeping Area:**
    - Designate a specific area for your dog's bed.
    - Choose a comfortable bed appropriate for the size of your dog.
    - Consider using a ticking clock or plush toy to comfort a puppy, mimicking the presence of its litter.

2. **Feeding Station:**
    - Set up a dedicated feeding area with food and water bowls.
    - Use sturdy, non-tip bowls to avoid spills.
    - Consider using a ceramic water bowl to keep water cooler and cleaner.

3. **Safety Measures:**
    - Secure any loose wires and cords that your dog might chew on.
    - Ensure that toxic plants are out of reach. Common toxic plants include lilies, azaleas, and Wandering Jew (which can irritate the skin).

- Remove or secure household chemicals, such as cleaning supplies, air fresheners, and pesticides.
- Check the yard for hazards like open pools, toxic plants, or small gaps in fencing where a dog could escape.

4. **Pet-Proofing Your Home:**
   - Move breakable items to higher shelves.
   - Install baby gates to restrict access to certain areas.
   - Ensure all trash cans have secure lids to prevent your dog from scavenging.

5. **Supplies:**
   - Purchase a collar and leash suitable for the dog's size and breed.
   - Have a variety of toys ready, such as rope toys and balls, to keep your dog entertained.
   - Provide appropriate chew toys to prevent destructive chewing.

6. **Grooming Essentials:**
   - Stock up on grooming supplies, including a brush, comb, and dog-specific shampoo.
   - Regular grooming helps maintain your dog's coat and overall health.

7. **Training Tools:**
   - Have training treats on hand to reward good behaviour.
   - Consider getting a crate for crate training, which can help with housebreaking and provide a safe space for your dog.

8. **Emergency Contacts:**
   - Prepare a list of emergency contacts, including local veterinarians and animal emergency clinics.
   - Share this information with family members or friends who may be responsible for your dog in your absence.

Creating a Safe and Comfortable Environment

1. **Establish Boundaries:**
   - Determine which areas of the house are off-limits to your dog and set up barriers if necessary.
   - Consistently enforce these boundaries from day one to avoid confusion.

2. **Routine and Structure:**
   - Establish a daily routine for feeding, walking, and playtime.
   - Consistent routines help dogs feel secure and understand what is expected of them.

3. **Gradual Introduction:**
   - Allow your dog to explore its new environment gradually.
   - Supervise interactions with other pets and family members to ensure they go smoothly.

4. **Comfort and Security:**
   - Provide a safe and quiet space for your dog to retreat to when feeling overwhelmed.

- Avoid overwhelming your new dog with too many new experiences at once.

5. **Health and Hygiene:**
    - Regularly clean your dog's living area and feeding station.
    - Monitor your dog's health by checking for signs of illness or discomfort.

By preparing your home thoroughly, you create a welcoming and safe environment for your new dog, helping them to adjust more quickly and comfortably. This preparation not only benefits your dog but also sets the stage for a successful and joyful pet ownership experience.

3

Essential Pre-Adoption Health Checks

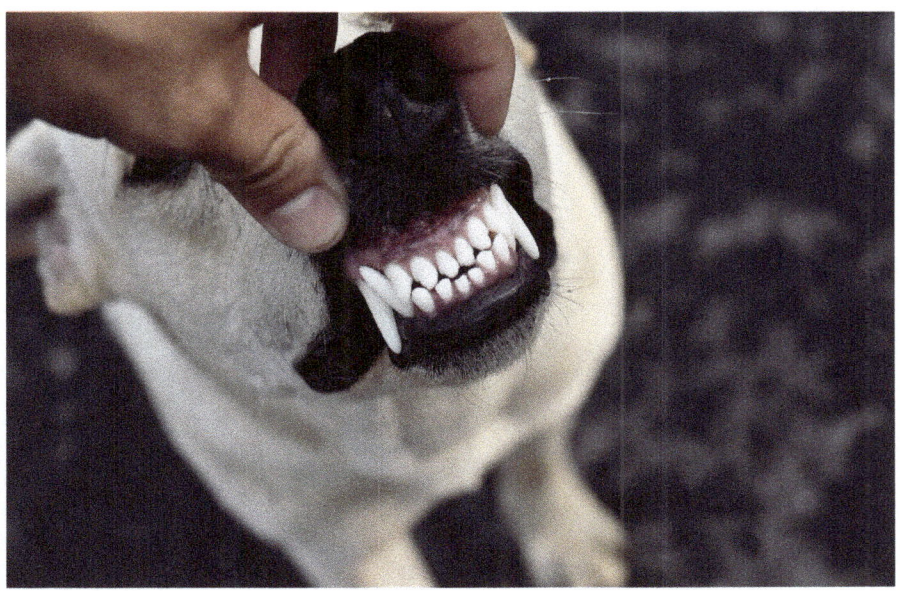

Acquiring a new dog is an exciting time, but it's essential to ensure that your new companion is healthy from the start. Performing health checks before bringing a dog home can save you from unexpected costs, potential health threats, and emotional distress. Imagine the scenario: You fall in love with a puppy that has an extended belly, which the breeder assures you is due to a recent meal. However, shortly after bringing the puppy home, it becomes very sick. A visit to the vet reveals the puppy is riddled with worms, leading to costly treatments and potential health risks to your family. This could have been avoided with a simple health check and asking the right questions.

Conducting Health Checks

General Appearance and Behaviour

- **Alertness and Activity:**
    - The dog should be alert, active, and interested in its surroundings.
    - Look for signs of lethargy or disinterest, which could indicate underlying health issues.

- **Coat Condition:**
    - A healthy dog has a shiny, smooth coat without bald patches or excessive shedding.
    - Check for signs of fleas, ticks, or skin irritations.

Eyes, Ears, and Mouth

- **Eyes:**
    - Eyes should be clear, bright, and free from discharge.
    - Look for redness, cloudiness, or excessive tearing.

- **Ears:**
    - Ears should be clean and odour-free. Any discharge or foul smell can indicate infections or mites.

- o Check for signs of ear mites, such as excessive scratching or head shaking.

- **Mouth:**
  - o Gums should be pink and moist, not pale or swollen.
  - o Teeth should be clean without excessive tartar buildup. Bad breath can indicate dental disease or other health issues.

Body and Limbs

- **Weight and Body Condition:**
  - o The dog should have a healthy weight. Ribs should be palpable but not visible.
  - o Check for any unusual lumps or bumps on the body.

- **Limbs and Mobility:**
  - o Observe the dog's movement. It should walk and run without limping or stiffness.
  - o Check the paws and nails for any injuries or abnormalities.

Abdomen and Genitals

- **Abdomen:**
  - o The belly should be soft and not overly bloated. A distended abdomen can indicate worms or other internal issues.
  - o Gently palpate the abdomen to check for tenderness or pain.

- **Genitals:**
    - The genital area should be clean and free from discharge or swelling.
    - Inspect for any signs of infection or abnormal growths.

Tail and Anal Area

- **Tail:**
    - The tail should be held normally and be free from any injuries or signs of discomfort.

- **Anal Area:**
    - The area around the anus should be clean and dry. Any signs of diarrhea or parasites should be noted.
    - Check for any lumps or growths that could indicate health issues.

Asking the Right Questions

- **Breeder or Shelter Background:**
    - Ask about the dog's medical history, including vaccinations and any previous illnesses.
    - Inquire about the dog's parents and any known genetic issues.

- **Behavioural History:**
    - Understand the dog's temperament and any known behavioural issues.
    - Ask about the dog's socialization and interaction with other animals and people.

Taking the time to perform these simple health checks can save you from unexpected expenses and potential heartache. A thorough examination helps ensure that your new dog is healthy and sets the foundation for a happy life together. Armed with these tips, you can confidently assess the health of your prospective pet, avoiding disappointment and ensuring a smoother transition into your home. Ensuring your new companion is healthy from the start is the first step in responsible pet ownership, leading to a rewarding and joyful experience.

4

Settling In – Helping your Dog Adjust to its New Home

Bringing a new dog into your home is an exciting time, but it can also be a bit overwhelming for both you and your new furry friend. Ensuring a smooth transition involves careful planning and patience, helping your dog feel safe and comfortable in its new environment. This chapter focuses on the steps to take from the moment you bring your new dog home to the first few weeks of settling in.

The Car Trip Home

The journey home is your dog's first experience with you as its new owner. Make it as calm and comfortable as possible.

- **Secure Transport:**
    - Use a crate or a car harness to keep your dog secure during the trip.
    - Bring a soft blanket or toy from the breeder or shelter to provide a familiar scent.

- **Calm Atmosphere:**
    - Keep the car ride smooth and quiet. Avoid loud music or sudden movements.
    - Speak softly and reassuringly to your dog.

Introducing Family Members

Introducing your new dog to family members should be done calmly and gradually.

- **Controlled Introduction:**
    - Have family members sit quietly and allow the dog to approach them at its own pace.
    - Avoid overwhelming the dog with too many people at once.

- **Positive Reinforcement:**
  - Use treats and praise to create positive associations with new people.
  - Encourage gentle petting and avoid sudden movements.

Exploring the New Environment

Allow your dog to explore its new home gradually to avoid overwhelming it.

- **Supervised Exploration:**
  - Let your dog explore one room at a time under supervision.
  - Keep doors to off-limit areas closed to prevent accidents.

- **Safe Space:**
  - Set up a designated area with your dog's bed, food, and water bowls.
  - Provide a quiet and comfortable space where the dog can retreat if feeling overwhelmed.

Establishing Boundaries and Routines

From the start, establish clear boundaries and routines to help your dog understand its place in the household.

- **Consistent Rules:**
  - Decide on household rules (e.g., no dogs on the sofa) and enforce them consistently from day one.

- o Ensure all family members are on the same page to avoid confusing the dog.

- **Daily Routine:**
  - o Establish a routine for feeding, walking, and playtime.
  - o Consistent routines help your dog feel secure and understand what to expect.

Comfort and Security

Creating a comfortable and secure environment is key to helping your dog settle in.

- **Comfortable Bedding:**
  - o Provide a cosy bed in a quiet area of the house.
  - o Include familiar items like a blanket or toy from the breeder or shelter.

- **Gradual Adjustment:**
  - o Avoid overwhelming your dog with too many new experiences at once.
  - o Gradually introduce new toys, activities, and environments.

Interaction with Other Pets

If you have other pets, introduce them to your new dog carefully and gradually.

- **Neutral Territory:**
  - Conduct initial introductions in a neutral space, like a backyard, to avoid territorial behaviour.

- **Supervised Interactions:**
  - Monitor all interactions closely to ensure they are positive and calm.
  - Separate the animals if there are any signs of aggression or stress.

Transitioning a new dog into your home requires patience, consistency, and understanding. By providing a calm and secure environment, establishing clear rules and routines, and gradually introducing your dog to its new surroundings and family members, you can help your new pet feel safe and loved. These steps will set the foundation for a happy and harmonious life together. Remember, the effort you put into this transition period will pay off in a well-adjusted and contented companion.

5
Basic Training and Ongoing Education

Training is a vital part of ensuring your dog grows up to be well-behaved and happy. Dogs are intelligent creatures that require both mental and physical stimulation, and training provides an excellent way to meet these needs.

The Importance of Training

Training your dog is not just about teaching commands; it's about building a strong bond and ensuring your dog can behave appropriately in various situations. Proper training helps prevent behavioural issues and makes life more enjoyable for both you and your dog.

Basic Commands

Starting with basic commands is essential for any dog, regardless of age. Consistency from all household members is key.

1. Sit:

- One of the most basic commands that can help control your dog in various situations.
- **Method:** Hold a treat above the dog's head and move it back slowly. As the dog follows the treat, it will naturally sit. Reward and praise immediately.

2. Stay:

- Useful for keeping your dog in one place and preventing unwanted behaviour.
- **Method:** Once the dog knows "sit," tell them to stay, step back, and if they remain in place, reward and praise them.

3. Come:

- Essential for recall and ensuring your dog returns to you in various situations.

- **Method:** Use a cheerful tone, say "come," and reward the dog when it approaches you.

4. Down:

- Helps in managing the dog in more relaxed situations.
- **Method:** Hold a treat in your hand, lower it to the ground, and move it away slowly. Reward when the dog lies down.

5. Leave It:

- Crucial for preventing your dog from picking up dangerous or unwanted items.
- **Method:** Hold a treat in both hands. Show one treat and say "leave it." When the dog ignores that hand, reward with the treat from the other hand.

The Importance of Consistency

Every member of the household must use the same commands and reward system to avoid confusing the dog. Consistent training sessions, using the same methods and commands, reinforce learning and good behaviour.

Advanced Training and Activities

Once basic commands are mastered, consider advanced training and activities to keep your dog mentally and physically stimulated.

1. Obedience Classes:

- Enrol in local obedience classes for structured training and socialisation.
- Suitable for dogs of all ages.

2. Agility Classes:

- Excellent for high-energy breeds needing physical exercise and mental challenges.
- Helps in building confidence and improving behaviour.

3. Working Dog Trials:

- Ideal for breeds with strong working instincts, such as herding or hunting.
- Provides an outlet for their natural behaviours in a controlled environment.

Addressing Behavioural Issues

1. Jumping on Visitors:

- Teach your dog to greet people politely. Use commands like "sit" or "stay" when visitors arrive and reward calm behaviour.

2. Barking:

- Identify the cause of barking (boredom, alert, anxiety) and address it accordingly. Training the "quiet" command can help manage excessive barking.

3. On-Leash Behaviour:

- Train your dog to walk on a leash without pulling. Use treats and praise to reward walking calmly beside you.

4. Off-Leash Behaviour:

- Ensure your dog has a reliable recall before allowing off-leash play. Practice in a safe, enclosed area and gradually increase the level of distractions.

Positive Reinforcement

Use treats and praise to reward good behaviour. Positive reinforcement is more effective than punishment, as it encourages the dog to repeat desired behaviours. Remember, smacking or yelling at your dog can lead to fear and aggression, making behavioural issues worse.

Training is a continuous process that requires patience, consistency, and dedication. By teaching basic commands, addressing behavioural issues promptly, and involving the whole family in the training process, you can ensure your dog grows up to be a well-behaved and happy companion. Enrol in obedience or agility classes to provide further stimulation and bonding opportunities. Remember, a well-trained dog is a joy to live with and reflects the care and commitment you invest in them.

6

Dogs and Children

Dogs and children can form wonderful bonds, but this relationship requires careful management and understanding. Many dogs end up being rehomed or worse due to misunderstandings or inappropriate interactions with children. It's crucial to educate both children and adults on how to interact with dogs responsibly and respectfully to ensure a harmonious household.

The Importance of Supervision and Education

Children can unintentionally cause stress or harm to dogs through pulling, poking, prodding, and screaming. This behaviour can lead to emotional stress and trauma for the dog and potential injuries for the child. Supervision and education are essential to foster a safe and respectful environment for both the child and the dog.

Common Issues and Solutions

1. Rough Handling and Inappropriate Play: Children often don't understand their own strength or the dog's fragility, especially with smaller breeds.

- **Solution:** Teach children to handle dogs gently, showing them how to pet softly and avoid rough play. Supervise all interactions to ensure the dog is not being hurt or stressed.

2. Loud Noises and Chaotic Environments: Arguments, yelling, and loud play can be very stressful for dogs.

- **Solution:** Create a calm environment around the dog. Explain to children how loud noises can scare and upset their pet.

3. Staring Competitions: Children may engage in staring contests with dogs, which can be perceived as a challenge by the dog.

- **Solution:** Educate children that staring at a dog can be seen as threatening. Encourage them to look away if a dog seems uncomfortable.

4. Leaving Gates Open: An open gate can lead to a dog escaping and potentially getting lost or injured.

- **Solution:** Make it a rule that gates and doors are always closed. Teach children the importance of keeping the dog safe by securing exits.

5. Conflicting Commands: Different family members giving different commands can confuse the dog and lead to behavioural issues.

- **Solution:** Ensure everyone in the household is using the same commands and training methods. Consider attending training sessions as a family to reinforce consistency.

6. Offering Inappropriate Food: Children may offer dogs food that is unsuitable or dangerous.

- **Solution:** Educate children about what foods are safe for dogs and which ones are not. Make it clear that human snacks are off-limits.

Size and Breed Considerations

The size of the dog and the breed's temperament are critical factors to consider when there are children in the household.

- **Large Dogs:** Larger dogs can accidentally knock over small children, leading to injuries.

- **Solution:** Teach children to stand still when large dogs are around and avoid running or sudden movements that might excite the dog.
- **Small Dogs:** Smaller dogs can be easily injured by rough handling.
  - **Solution:** Supervise playtime to ensure the dog is not being handled too roughly. Teach children to be gentle and to give the dog space when needed.

Educating Children on Dog's Emotions

Dogs have emotions too, and it is essential for children to understand this. Teaching empathy can help children develop a deeper bond with their pet.

- **Solution:** Explain to children that dogs can feel scared, happy, sad, and excited just like humans. Encourage them to be aware of the dog's body language and to respect its feelings.

Training Together as a Family

Consistent training is crucial for a well-behaved dog, and involving the whole family ensures everyone is on the same page.

- **Solution:** Attend training sessions together and practice commands as a family. This consistency helps the dog learn faster and reduces confusion.

The Emotional Impact of Rehoming

When a dog is rehomed due to behavioural issues or poor breed choice, it can leave children feeling heartbroken, confused, and angry.

- **Solution:** Make informed decisions about breed selection and ensure the family is prepared for the responsibility. Discuss the commitment required and the potential challenges before bringing a dog home.

Integrating a dog into a family with children requires education, supervision, and consistent training. By teaching children to interact with dogs respectfully and understanding the dog's needs and emotions, you can foster a safe and loving environment for both. This approach not only benefits the dog but also helps children develop empathy and responsibility. Remember, a well-informed and prepared family creates a happy and harmonious life for their canine companion.

7
Keeping your Dog Happy and Healthy

Owning a dog is a long-term commitment that goes beyond the initial excitement of bringing a new pet home. As time passes, it is easy to become complacent, but your dog's health and happiness depend on consistent care. Regular maintenance helps prevent health issues, ensures your dog stays active and engaged, and strengthens the bond between you and your pet. It's a tragedy when a dog, once loved, becomes neglected or forgotten, so it's vital to keep the love and care consistent throughout the dog's life.

Diet and Nutrition

Proper nutrition is the foundation of good health for your dog. A balanced diet supports growth, energy levels, and overall well-being.

Puppies:

- Puppies require smaller, more frequent meals to support their rapid growth and high energy levels.
- As the puppy grows, gradually reduce the number of meals to twice a day by adulthood.

Adult Dogs:

- Adult dogs need a balanced diet that includes proteins, fats, carbohydrates, vitamins, and minerals.
- Adjust portion sizes based on your dog's activity level, breed, and size to prevent obesity.

Senior Dogs:

- Older dogs may require diets with higher fibre content and lower calories to maintain a healthy weight.
- Senior dogs might benefit from additional supplements like glucosamine for joint health.

Special Diets:

- Some dogs have specific dietary needs due to allergies or medical conditions. Consult a professional for tailored advice.

Exercise and Mental Stimulation

Exercise is essential for your dog's physical health, while mental stimulation keeps them engaged and prevents boredom.

Physical Exercise:

- Regular walks, playtime, and exercise help maintain a healthy weight and prevent obesity.
- High-energy breeds may require more vigorous activities, such as running or agility training.

Mental Stimulation:

- Interactive toys, puzzle feeders, and training sessions keep your dog's mind sharp.
- Agility trials, working dog trials, and obedience classes provide excellent mental and physical stimulation.

Consistency:

- It's important to maintain regular exercise routines. Consistent physical and mental stimulation prevents behavioural issues and keeps your dog happy and healthy.

Grooming and Hygiene

Regular grooming is vital for maintaining your dog's coat and overall health. The grooming needs vary by breed, and it's crucial to understand these requirements.

Coat Care:

- **Short-haired Breeds:** Regular brushing with a rubber mitt stimulates the skin and keeps the coat shiny.
- **Long-haired Breeds:** Daily brushing prevents mats and tangles. Tools like de-matting combs and de-shedding brushes are helpful.
- **Dogs with Skin Folds:** Breeds like Bulldogs and Shar-Peis need special attention to their skin folds to prevent infections.
- **Hairless Breeds:** Regular skin care and protection from the sun are essential.

Ear Care:

- Regularly check your dog's ears for signs of infection or mites. Clean with a cloth and a bit of coconut oil on a tissue.
- Dogs with floppy ears are more prone to ear infections and need more frequent checks.

Dental Care:

- Natural methods like raw bones, rope toys, and dental chews help keep your dog's teeth clean.
- Regular dental checks and cleaning are essential to prevent dental disease.

Tick and Flea Prevention:

- During grooming, check for ticks, fleas, and other parasites. Finding a tick too late can be fatal.
- Regular grooming reduces the risk of infestations and helps maintain a healthy coat.

Bathing:

- Bathe your dog as needed based on their activity level and coat type. Avoid using human shampoos and choose dog-specific products.
- Avoid over-bathing, as it can strip the natural oils from the coat, leaving the skin exposed and at risk of irritation and damage to the coat.

Emotional Well-being

Dogs have emotions, and it's important to cater to their emotional needs to ensure a balanced and happy life.

Love and Attention:

- Continue to show your dog love and attention throughout their life.
- Consistent interaction and affection prevent feelings of neglect and abandonment.

Training and Socialization:

- Ongoing training and socialization help maintain good behaviour and prevent anxiety.
- Family participation in training builds stronger bonds and ensures everyone is consistent with commands.

Maintaining a healthy dog involves a balanced diet, regular exercise, mental stimulation, and proper grooming. Understanding and catering to your dog's changing needs as they age ensures they remain happy and healthy. Consistent care prevents health issues and behavioural problems, fostering a strong bond between you and your pet. By committing to your dog's well-being, you ensure they live a fulfilling and joyous life, reflecting the love and care they receive from you.

8

Signs of Illness and When to Seek Help

As a responsible pet owner, it's crucial to monitor your dog's health and behaviour closely. Early detection of signs of illness can prevent minor issues from becoming severe problems. Being vigilant and proactive in seeking help ensures your dog does not suffer unnecessarily. Remember, the dog is the one who suffers if their health needs are ignored, so it's essential to act promptly.

Common Signs of Illness:

1. **Behavioural Changes:**
   - Lethargy, increased aggression, or withdrawal can indicate illness or pain.
   - Changes in appetite or drinking habits should be noted.

2. **Gastrointestinal Issues:**
   - Vomiting, diarrhea, or constipation can be signs of digestive problems or infections.
   - Observe for any blood in stools or unusual bowel movements.

3. **Respiratory Problems:**
   - Coughing, wheezing, or difficulty breathing can indicate respiratory infections or other issues.
   - Persistent sneezing or nasal discharge should be checked.

4. **Skin and Coat Issues:**
   - Persistent itching, redness, or hair loss can be signs of allergies, parasites, or skin infections.
   - Check for lumps, bumps, or sores on the skin.

5. **Eye and Ear Problems:**
   - Red, swollen, or discharge from eyes and ears can indicate infections.
   - Changes in vision or hearing should be monitored.

When to Seek Help:

1. **Emergencies:**
   - For severe symptoms like difficulty breathing, seizures, or uncontrolled bleeding, seek immediate help.
   - In cases of suspected poisoning or ingestion of toxic substances, contact an emergency clinic or poison control immediately.

2. **Professional Consultation:**
   - Consult a pet behaviorist or a professional for persistent behavioural issues or signs of pain.
   - Regular health checks by a professional can help detect and manage potential health problems early.

Toxic Reactions and Allergies:

1. **Vaccine Reactions:**
   - Watch for signs of vaccine reactions such as swelling, lethargy, or fever within 48 hours of vaccination.
   - Seek help if symptoms persist or worsen.

2. **Allergies:**
   - Common signs of allergies include itching, redness, and gastrointestinal issues.
   - Identify and eliminate allergens from your dog's environment and diet.

Specific Health Issues:

1. **Tick Paralysis:**
   - Symptoms include weakness, paralysis, and breathing difficulties.
   - Remove ticks promptly and seek help if symptoms appear.

2. **Middle Ear Infections:**
   - Signs include head shaking, scratching at the ears, and balance issues.
   - Clean ears regularly and seek help if an infection is suspected.

3. **Snake Bites:**
   - Symptoms include swelling, pain, and lethargy.
   - Photograph the snake if possible and seek immediate help.

4. **Snail and Rodent Baits:**
   - Symptoms of poisoning include vomiting, seizures, and bleeding.
   - Keep baits out of reach and seek help if poisoning is suspected.

5. **Spider Bites:**
   - Symptoms include swelling, pain, and lethargy.
   - Monitor the bite site and seek help if symptoms worsen.

Emotional Trauma:

1. **Shock Symptoms:**
   - Signs include rapid breathing, pale gums, and weakness.
   - Keep the dog calm and seek help immediately.

2. **Behavioural Changes:**
   - Emotional trauma can manifest as fear, aggression, or withdrawal.
   - Consult a professional for behavioural therapy and support.

Monitoring your dog's health and recognizing signs of illness early is crucial for their well-being. Always keep emergency contact numbers readily available—in your wallet, car, home, and workplace—so you are prepared for any situation. It's better to have a false alarm than a fatality, so never hesitate to reach out for help if you notice something amiss. Prioritizing your dog's health and acting promptly can make all the difference in ensuring a happy, healthy life for your beloved companion. Remember, your vigilance and preparedness are key to your dog's well-being.

9

Recommended Reading and Resources

Expanding your knowledge about dogs and pet care is crucial for responsible pet ownership. The following books and resources offer valuable insights into various aspects of dog care, training, health, and overall well-being. These recommendations will provide you with additional guidance and support on your journey to becoming a knowledgeable and compassionate dog owner.

Books

1. **What Vets Don't Tell You About Vaccines by Catherine O'Driscoll**
   - A comprehensive guide that discusses the potential risks and benefits of vaccinations for pets, offering an alternative perspective on traditional veterinary practices.

     https://www.catherineodriscoll.com/what-vets-dont-tell-you- about-vaccines.html

2. **Who's the Boss by Val Bonney**
   - This book provides practical advice on training your dog and establishing yourself as the pack leader, ensuring a harmonious relationship between you and your pet.

     https://www.bonnies.com.au/product-page/who-s-the-boss-book

3. **Give Your Dog a Bone by Dr. Ian Billinghurst**
   - Focuses on the benefits of a raw food diet for dogs, explaining how natural feeding practices can promote better health and longevity.

     https://drianbillinghurst.com/product/give-your-dog-a-bone/

4. **The Encyclopedia of Natural Pet Care by CJ Puotinen**
   - A thorough resource on natural and holistic approaches to pet care, covering everything from diet and nutrition to herbal remedies and alternative therapies.

Training Resources

1. **Graeme Hall (The Dogfather)**
   - Although Graeme Hall does not have a specific book, his training methods and advice can be found on his website and through his television programs.

     https://www.dogfather.co.uk/

2. **Cesar Millan**
   - Known for his expertise in dog psychology and training, Cesar Millan offers numerous resources through his books, television shows, and online content.

     https://www.cesarmillan.com/

Conclusion

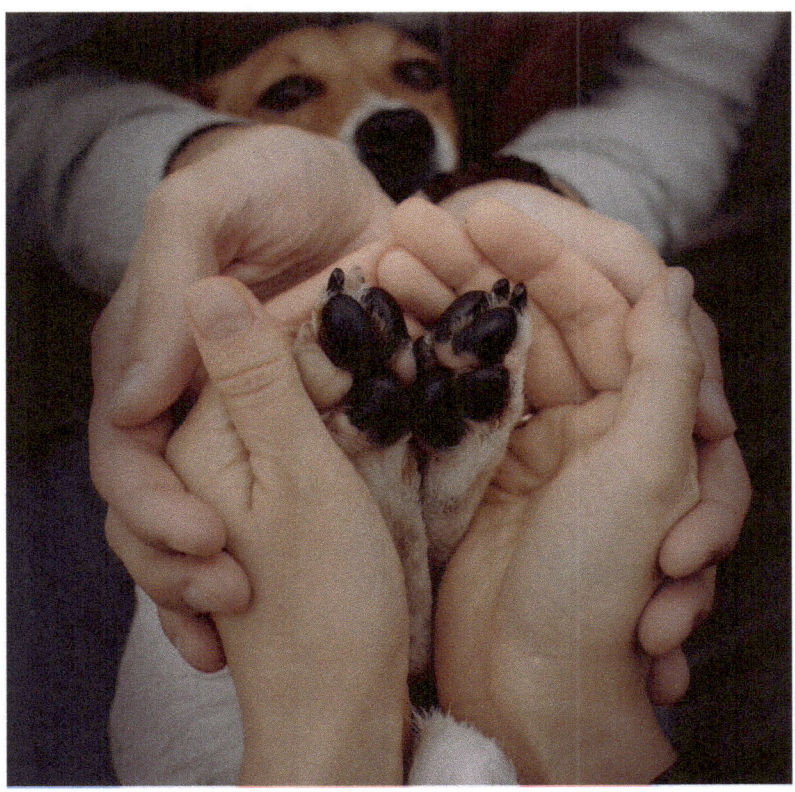

Thank you for taking the time to read this book. By doing so, you've taken the first step towards becoming a responsible pet owner. Owning a dog is a significant commitment, and it is crucial to consider every aspect to ensure a happy, healthy, and fulfilling life for your new companion.

If you need further information or guidance on any of the subjects covered in this book, please don't hesitate to reach out. I offer Zoom consultations worldwide to provide personalized advice and support. Making the right decision is essential for both you and your dog, as it ensures a harmonious and joyful relationship for everyone involved.

I hope this book has provided you with valuable insights and practical advice to help you make informed decisions about selecting and caring for your dog. Congratulations on your journey in welcoming a new dog into your life. Together, we can make a difference and create a world where every pet has a loving, permanent home.

For more information or to schedule a consultation, visit [Majella's Pet Store](#).

Warm regards,

Majella

Legal Notice

Title: *So, You Want to Get a Dog?*
Author: Majella Gee
Publisher: Sorjam Publishing
ISBN: 978-1-7636631-2-1

Copyright © 2024 by Majella Gee. All rights reserved.

No part of this book may be reproduced, distributed, or transmitted in any form or by any means, including photocopying, recording, or other electronic or mechanical methods, without the prior written permission of the publisher, except in the case of brief quotations embodied in critical reviews and certain other non-commercial uses permitted by copyright law. For permission requests, write to the publisher, addressed "Attention: Permissions Coordinator," at the address below.

Publisher Contact Information:

Sorjam Publishing

Email: hello@majellaspetstore.com
Website: https://majellaspetstore.com/

This book is a work of nonfiction. The events described in this book are based on real-life experiences, but the names, locations, and identifying details have been changed to protect the privacy of individuals. Any similarity to real persons, living or dead, is purely coincidental.

Disclaimer:

The information provided in this book is for educational purposes only and is not intended as a substitute for professional veterinary advice, diagnosis, or treatment. Always seek the advice of your veterinarian or other qualified pet care professional with any questions you may have regarding the health or behaviour of your pet. Reliance on any information provided in this book is solely at your own risk.

The publisher and author assume no responsibility or liability for any damages or injuries arising from the use of or reliance on the information provided in this book.

Trademark Notice:

All product names, logos, and brands mentioned in this book are property of their respective owners. All company, product, and service names used in this book are for identification purposes only. Use of these names, logos, and brands does not imply endorsement.

www.ingramcontent.com/pod-product-compliance
Lightning Source LLC
Chambersburg PA
CBHW061212070526
44583CB00025B/3214